CONTEÚDO DIGITAL PARA ALUNOS

Cadastre-se e transforme seus estudos em uma experiência única de aprendizado:

Entre na página de cadastro:

https://sistemas.editoradobrasil.com.br/cadastro

Além dos seus dados pessoais e dos dados de sua escola, adicione ao cadastro o código do aluno, que garantirá a exclusividade do seu ingresso à plataforma.

1261737A1001358

CB015197

Depois, acesse:

https://leb.editoradobrasil.com.br/

e navegue pelos conteúdos digitais de sua coleção :D

Lembre-se de que esse código, pessoal e intransferível, é valido por um ano. Guarde-o com cuidado, pois é a única maneira de você acessar os conteúdos da plataforma.

Editora do Brasil

BRINCANDO
COM INGLÊS

3

ENSINO FUNDAMENTAL
ANOS INICIAIS

RENATO MENDES CURTO JÚNIOR

Licenciado em Letras

Certificado de proficiência em Língua Inglesa pela Universidade de Michigan e TOEFL

Autor de livros de educação a distância

Professor de Língua Inglesa e Portuguesa na rede particular de ensino desde 1986

ANNA CAROLINA GUIMARÃES

Licenciada em pedagogia

Especialista em Educação Infantil e anos iniciais

Especialista em neuropsicopedagogia

Coordenadora pedagógica de Educação básica

CIBELE MENDES

Mestre em Educação

Licenciada em Pedagogia

Certificado de proficiência em Língua Inglesa pela Fluency Academy

Coordenadora pedagógica de Educação Infantil aos Anos Finais do Ensino Fundamental

Editora
do Brasil

Dados Internacionais de Catalogação na Publicação (CIP)
(Câmara Brasileira do Livro, SP, Brasil)

Curto Júnior, Renato Mendes
    Brincando com inglês 3 : ensino fundamental :
anos iniciais / Renato Mendes Curto Júnior, Anna
Carolina Guimarães, Cibele Mendes. -- 5. ed. --
São Paulo : Editora do Brasil, 2024. -- (Brincando
com)

    ISBN 978-85-10-09498-6 (aluno)
    ISBN 978-85-10-09499-3 (professor)

    1. Língua inglesa (Ensino fundamental)
I. Guimarães, Anna Carolina. II. Mendes, Cibele.
III. Título. IV. Série.

24-197237   CDD-372.652

Índices para catálogo sistemático:

1. Língua inglesa : Ensino fundamental 372.652
Cibele Maria Dias - Bibliotecária - CRB-8/9427

Direção-geral: Paulo Serino de Souza

Diretoria editorial: Felipe Ramos Poletti
Gerência editorial de conteúdo didático: Erika Caldin
Gerência editorial de produção e design: Ulisses Pires
Supervisão de design: Aurélio Gadini Camilo
Supervisão de arte: Abdonildo José de Lima Santos
Supervisão de revisão: Elaine Silva
Supervisão de iconografia: Léo Burgos
Supervisão de digital: Priscila Hernandez
Supervisão de controle e planejamento editorial: Roseli Said
Supervisão de direitos autorais: Jennifer Xavier

Supervisão editorial: Carla Felix Lopes e Diego Mata
Edição: Danuza D. Gonçalves, Graziele Arantes Mattiuzzi, Natália Feulo,
Nayra Simões e Sheila Fabre.
Assistência editorial: Igor Gonçalves, Julia do Nascimento e Pedro Andrade Bezerra
Revisão: 2014 Soluções Editoriais, Alexander Siqueira, Andréia Andrade, Beatriz Dorini,
Gabriel Ornelas, Jonathan Busato, Júlia Castelo Branco, Mariana Paixão, Martin Gonçalves,
Rita Costa, Rosani Andreani e Sandra Fernandes
Pesquisa iconográfica: Maria Santos e Selma Nagano
Tratamento de imagens: Robson Mereu
Projeto gráfico: Caronte Design
Capa: Caronte Design
Imagem de capa: Thais Castro
Edição de arte: Camila de Camargo e Marcos Gubiotti
Ilustrações: André Aguiar, Bruna Ishihara, Carolina Sartório, Dayane Raven, Desenhorama,
Evandro Marenda, Janete Trindade, Luiz Lentini, Maíra Nakazaki, Marcos de Mello,
Reinaldo Rosa, Vanessa Alexandre e Vinicius Meneghin
Editoração eletrônica: Abel Design
Licenciamentos de textos: Cinthya Utiyama, Jennifer Xavier, Paula Harue Tozaki
e Renata Garbellini
Controle e planejamento editorial: Ana Fernandes, Bianca Gomes, Juliana Gonçalves,
Maria Trofino, Terezinha Oliveira e Valéria Alves

5ª edição / 1ª impressão, 2024
Impresso na Hawaii Gráfica e Editora

**Editora
do Brasil**

Avenida das Nações Unidas, 12901
Torre Oeste, 20º andar
São Paulo, SP – CEP: 04578-910
Fone: + 55 11 3226-0211
www.editoradobrasil.com.br

ASSOCIAÇÃO
BRASILEIRA
DOS DIREITOS
REPROGRÁFICOS

Respeite o direito autoral

APRESENTAÇÃO

Querido aluno, querida aluna,

Este material foi elaborado para que você aprenda inglês de forma divertida, por meio de atividades estimulantes e desafiadoras, com o intuito de transformar a sala de aula em um espaço para praticar a língua inglesa brincando!

Nesta nova versão do **Brincando com Inglês**, cada aula será uma nova experiência, e você não vai querer parar de aprender. Vamos começar?

Os autores

CONHEÇA SEU LIVRO

Boas-vindas à nova edição do **Brincando com Inglês**!

LET'S START!

No início de cada volume, esta seção apresenta atividades lúdicas que possibilitam a preparação para os novos conteúdos, resgatando conhecimentos prévios.

COMPREHENSION

As atividades desta seção visam à compreensão do texto visto na abertura da unidade.

VOCABULARY

Apresenta o vocabulário das palavras vistas na unidade, com a tradução em língua portuguesa.

LET'S PLAY

Seção relacionada aos conceitos propostos e à temática da unidade. Você encontrará atividades lúdicas, como diagrama de palavras, jogos de relacionar, jogos de erros, desafios etc.

LET'S LISTEN

Seção com atividades que têm como objetivo a compreensão de áudios.

LET'S HAVE FUN

Localizada no final das unidades, contém atividades variadas cuja proposta é desenvolver o estudo da língua inglesa com atividades práticas, ampliando o conhecimento e o vocabulário trabalhado.

LET'S SING!

Músicas para os alunos cantarem e praticarem o vocabulário visto na unidade de forma lúdica e divertida.

GOOD DEED

Apresenta atividades temáticas de cunho social e ético relacionadas ao assunto de cada unidade. Aborda as competências gerais e socioemocionais da BNCC e as atividades feitas em grupo ou em dupla.

GRAMMAR POINT

Boxe com conteúdos gramaticais para que você compreenda a estrutura estudada e sistematize escrita e oralidade.

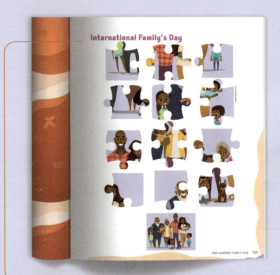

CELEBRATIONS

Encartes com atividades relacionadas a datas comemorativas.

ENGLISH AROUND THE WORLD

Seção que contempla a dimensão intercultural da língua inglesa, trabalhando elementos da cultura em que se fala o idioma como língua oficial ou franca. Também são estudados os aspectos interculturais de outros países.

DIGITAL PLAY

Seção que traz atividades em que se usa a tecnologia: filmagem, fotos, uso de apps e jogos *on-line*.

STICKERS

Adesivos para colar em algumas atividades.

AFTER THIS UNIT I CAN

Seção de autoavaliação.

ÍCONES

 ADESIVO

 APONTAR

 CANTAR

 CARTONADO

 CIRCULAR

 COLAR

 COLORIR

 CONTAR

 DESENHAR

 ENCONTRAR/PESQUISAR

 FALAR OU CONVERSAR

 LIGAR/RELACIONAR

 MARCAR

 RECORTAR

 TRAÇAR/ESCREVER

CONTENTS

LET'S START!

1 What's your favorite color? Write and stamp your finger.

Add your
stamp here

My favorite color is 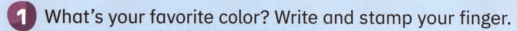.

2 What is your name?

My name is 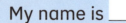.

3 What is your friend's name?

My friend's name is 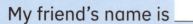.

4 What's your favorite day of the week?

My favorite day of the week is .

5 Write down the days of the week in the correct order.

6 Complete the calendar. Then paste the sticker on your birthday date.

SUN	MON	TUE	WED	THU	FRI	SAT

_____	_____
cars	colored pencils
_____	_____
T-shirts	spinning tops
_____	_____
pairs of socks	books

8 Find the names of some school objects in the wordsearch.

Dr. Norbert Lange/Shutterstock.com

Sompong maleehuan/Shutterstock.com

Guki/Shutterstock.com

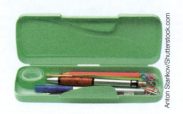
Anton Starikov/Shutterstock.com

Mega Pixel/Shutterstock.com

MeteeChaicharoen/Shutterstock.com

karen roach/Shutterstock.com

feeling lucky/Shutterstock.com

Y	B	O	O	K	F	G	H	J	K	L	Ç	M	N	B
V	C	X	Z	A	M	N	B	V	C	X	Z	Ç	K	L
J	H	G	P	E	N	C	I	L	*	C	A	S	E	D
T	Y	J	M	N	J	I	O	U	A	E	I	X	A	E
Q	B	A	C	K	P	A	C	K	E	R	L	N	D	R
A	T	G	K	L	E	F	A	C	X	F	K	B	U	A
Z	S	H	A	R	P	E	N	E	R	V	P	V	P	S
X	R	B	I	O	H	K	L	M	O	B	O	*	O	E
S	P	E	N	C	I	L	A	E	D	H	I	S	L	R
W	E	N	U	P	A	J	L	*	G	Y	U	D	A	Z
E	N	H	J	L	D	Q	E	T	U	O	P	S	F	H
C	V	Y	H	N	O	T	E	B	O	O	K	T	Q	E

9 Color the ice cream cones according to the labels.

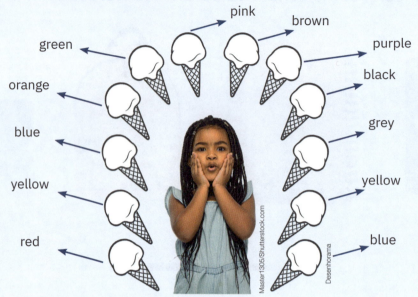

pink

brown

green

purple

black

orange

blue

grey

yellow

yellow

red

blue

10 Match each word to the corresponding picture.

a) Invitation

b) Birthday cake

c) Party

HAPPY BIRTHDAY

LEVEL UP
BIRTHDAY PARTY
YOU'RE INVITED
Chris's 10th Birthday Celebration

d) Friend

 January

 March

 May

 July

 September

 November

katarina_1/Shutterstock.com

12 Look at the pictures and circle the corresponding word.

Theater
Hospital
Park

Supermarket
Bakery
Bus stop

School
Library
Restaurant

Fire station
Museum
Bank

Museum
Bank
Supermarket

Park
Bus stop
School

Bus stop
Fire station
Library

Hospital
Park
Fire station

Bakery
Museum
Hospital

Library
Supermarket
Theater

IT'S TIME FOR GOOD THINGS!

Vanessa Alexandre

VOCABULARY

Creative: criativo(a).

Excited: animada(o).

Fun: divertido.

Good things: coisas boas.

Grateful: agradecida(o).

Happy: feliz.

Hello: Olá!

I feel: Eu me sinto.

Music class: aula de música.

Musical instrument(s): instrumento(s) musical(is).

Play music (to play): toco música (tocar).

School band: banda da escola.

Today: hoje.

What's up?: E aí?

1 Why are the children happy? Check the correct answer to complete the sentence.

Because they have... today.

⊠

☐ Gym class

☐ Science class

☐ Music class

2 Where are the children playing music? Check.   ⊠

☐ In a theater.   ☐ In a classroom.   ☐ In a garden.

3 Answer the following questions.   ✏️

a) How many people are there in the Music class?

_____

b) Who is very happy and excited?

_____

c) What did Lisa say?

_____

1 Complete the crossword.

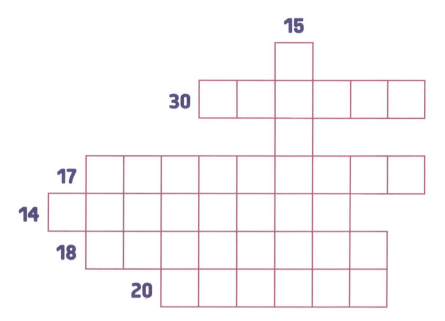

2 Write the words from the box in the appropriate place.

students

teacher

school

music

classroom

a) It's so fun. I feel grateful to be in the _____ band.

b) My _____ is a special musician.

c) The _____ love to play _____ and feel creative.

d) We play musical instruments in our _____.

Look at the pictures and find the corresponding words in the wordsearch.

Z	X	P	C	V	B	B	N	M	L	K	J	H	P	F	G
R	D	E	S	K	T	T	Y	U	I	O	X	P	E	S	A
A	S	N	C	I	L	I	S	H	A	R	P	E	N	E	R
H	J	K	L	K	H	T	F	S	Z	C	X	B	C	N	M
V	R	U	L	E	R	W	G	Y	J	B	X	A	I	D	N
M	L	K	F	R	N	R	M	L	K	O	O	N	L	L	O
U	I	O	S	A	P	P	U	I	O	O	O	Y	U	I	T
U	O	W	A	S	T	E	B	A	S	K	E	T	T	O	E
S	Z	C	N	E	F	J	O	K	C	S	D	F	S	Z	B
C	H	A	I	R	N	Z	A	M	K	H	*	W	N	F	O
F	D	D	F	D	D	O	R	R	D	E	E	D	F	D	O
A	D	F	D	D	F	*	D	D	F	L	K	D	F	D	K
M	N	V	X	Q	M	*	X	F	D	F	F	A	N	Q	M

1 Listen, complete, and color the objects.

a) This is a _____ window.

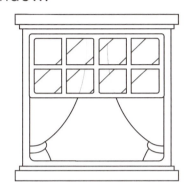

b) This is a _____ bookshelf.

c) This is a _____ board.

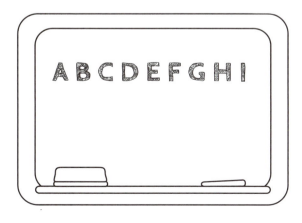

d) This is an _____ fan.

Ilustrações: Marcos de Mello

e) These are a _____ desk and a _____ chair.

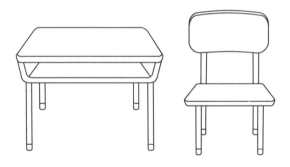

f) This is a _____ wastebasket.

Let's make a campaign to keep the school clean!

We should all keep the school clean and well organized.

1 Look at the picture and talk about it.

2 How can we keep the school clean? Check the correct options.

Classroom

There's a **desk**,
There's a **board**,
In the classroom,
In the classroom.

There's a **fan**,
There's a chair,
In the classroom,
In the classroom.

There's a **wastebasket**,
There's a **bookshelf**,
In the classroom,
In the classroom.

There are students,
There's a teacher,
In the school,
In the school.

Written especially for this book.

LET'S SING!

VOCABULARY

Board: lousa.
Bookshelf: estante.
Desk: carteira escolar.
Fan: ventilador.
Wastebasket: lixeira.

Marcos de Mello

Curiosities about transportation in the United States

Check the American school bus.

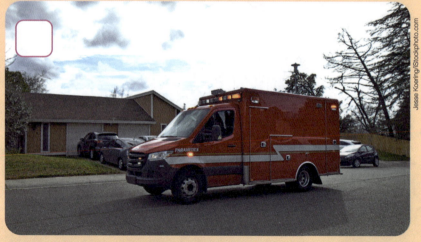

Wastage and the issue of garbage in the United States of America

Draw your own recycling symbol. Use your creativity.

LET'S PLAY

1 Match the musical note to the instruments. Then write down their names.

Vinicius Meneghin

_____   _____

_____   _____

_____   _____

2 How are you feeling today? Paste the stickers and circle your emotions.

angry

accomplished

calm

excited

happy

hurt

intelligent

shy

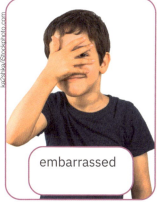
embarrassed

satisfied

funny

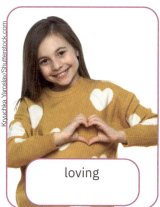
loving

3 Find the feelings in the wordsearch and paint.

happy ✳ intelligent ✳ thankful ✳ creative ✳ funny

V	C	H	A	P	P	Y	B	V	C	I	Z
J	H	G	L	S	N	C	O	L	M	N	W
T	Y	J	M	F	U	J	T	G	N	T	J
Q	Z	X	C	K	F	U	N	N	Y	E	L
A	T	G	K	L	E	X	Y	C	T	L	K
Z	T	H	A	N	K	F	U	L	T	L	P
X	R	B	I	O	H	K	L	M	O	I	O
C	R	E	A	T	I	V	E	E	D	G	I
W	H	N	U	P	A	J	L	P	G	E	U
E	N	H	J	L	D	Q	E	T	U	N	P
C	V	Y	H	W	D	D	E	N	K	T	K

AFTER THIS UNIT I CAN

Identify and name the feelings in English.

Identify good and positive actions.

Identify and name musical instruments in English.

Identify and add numbers.

Understand the importance of recycling.

Comprehend and identify good and bad choices.

UNIT
2
GAMES AND FUN

I **like** games. And you?

Me **too**! I **play** many **games**.

I **adore** **amusement parks**!

They're amazing! I like the roller coaster and the ferris wheel.

I like the ferris wheel, too!

Vanessa Alexandre

 VOCABULARY

Adore (to adore): adoro (adorar).

Amusement park(s): parque(s) de diversões.

Game(s): jogo(s).

Like (to like): gosto (gostar).

Play (to play): brinco (brincar).

Too: também.

1 What are the kids talking about? Check.

☐ School and lessons.   ☐ Amusement parks and games.

2 Which ride do you like? Roller coasters or ferris wheels?

Write the name and draw it in the box below.

_____

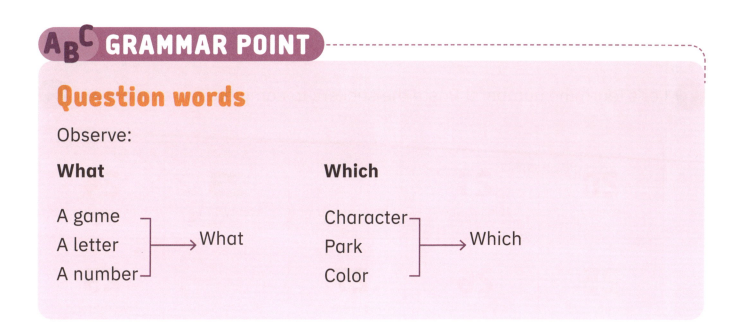

ABC GRAMMAR POINT

Question words

Observe:

What

A game
A letter → What
A number

Which

Character
Park → Which
Color

LET'S PLAY

1 Which games do you like to play?

☐ Bingo

☐ Electronic games

☐ Board games

☐ Cards

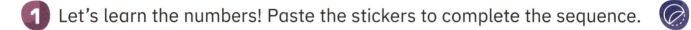
1 Let's learn the numbers! Paste the stickers to complete the sequence.

20 twenty	**21** twenty-one	twenty-two	**23** twenty-three	**24** twenty-four
25 twenty-five	**26** twenty-six	**27** twenty-seven	twenty-eight	**29** twenty-nine
30 thirty	thirty-one	**32** thirty-two	**33** thirty-three	thirty-four
35 thirty-five	**36** thirty-six	thirty-seven	**38** thirty-eight	**39** thirty-nine
forty	**41** forty-one	**42** forty-two	**43** forty-three	**44** forty-four
45 forty-five	**46** forty-six	**47** forty-seven	**48** forty-eight	**49** forty-nine
50 fifty	**51** fifty-one	fifty-two	**53** fifty-three	**54** fifty-four
55 fifty-five	**56** fifty-six	**57** fifty-seven	**58** fifty-eight	fifty-nine

2 Complete the words with the missing letters. Then match the words with the numbers.

t___e___ty   **39**

___w___nt___-t___o   **50**

t___e___ ___y-___iv___   **48**

t___i___t___-fo___r   **20**

___h___rt___-s___ve___   **56**

t___ ___rt___-n___n___   **43**

f___rt___-___n___   **25**

___o___ty-t___re___   **34**

___o___ty-e___g___t   **22**

fi___t___   **59**

f___f___y-si___   **41**

___ift___-___i___e   **37**

3 Complete the sequence with even numbers.

START

20 _____

21 twenty-one

22 _____

23 twenty-three

24 _____

25 twenty-five

26 _____

27 twenty-seven

28 _____

29 twenty-nine

30 _____

31 thirty-one

32 _____

33 thirty-three

34 _____

35 thirty-five

36 _____

37 thirty-seven

38 _____

39 thirty-nine

40 _____

41 forty-one

42 _____

43 forty-three

44 _____

45 forty-five

46 _____

47 forty-seven

48 _____

49 forty-nine

50 _____

51 fifty-one

52 _____

53 fifty-three

54 _____

55 fifty-five

56 _____

57 fifty-seven

58 _____

59 fifty-nine

FINISH

4 Find out the amusement park ride each child will go to. Write.

_____ _____   _____

Amusement parks

What kinds of toys are there in amusement parks? Check.

Dayane Raven

Hula-hoops: from Ancient Egypt to Global Crash

Number the correct image.

1 Children throwing hula-hoops.

2 Children rolling hula-hoops.

 **GOOD DEED**

Let's play cooperative games at school!

The students should always help friends to play.

What can you do to help your friends? Check the correct options.

a)

☐

c)

☐

b)

☐

d)

☐

Bingo

There was a **farmer who had** a dog,
and Bingo was his name-o.
B-I-N-G-O (3x)
And Bingo was his name-o.

There was a farmer who had a dog,
and Bingo was his name-o.
(**clap**)-I-N-G-O (3x)
And Bingo was his name-o.

 VOCABULARY

Clap (to clap): bata palmas (bater palmas).
Farmer: fazendeiro.
Had (to have): tinha (ter).
Who: que, quem.

There was a farmer who had a dog,
and Bingo was his name-o.
(clap)-(clap)-N-G-O (3x)
And Bingo was his name-o.

There was a farmer who had a dog,
and Bingo was his name-o.
(clap)-(clap)-(clap)-G-O (3x)
And Bingo was his name-o.

There was a farmer who had a dog,
and Bingo was his name-o.
(clap)-(clap)-(clap)-(clap)-O (3x)
And Bingo was his name-o.

There was a farmer who had a dog,
and Bingo was his name-o.
(clap)-(clap)-(clap)-(clap)-(clap) (3x)
And Bingo was his name-o.

Folk song.

Marcos de Mello

1 Listen and answer.

Letter I, number 20!

Congratulations, Stephany!

Bingo!

Vanessa Alexandre

a) Who is feeling lucky? Circle.

Ilustrações: Vanessa Alexandre

b) How many numbers did they mark? Match.

Lisa   one

Dylan   all

Stephany   three

c) Which number did Stephany need?

☐ Twenty.

☐ Twelve.

2 Listen, complete, and draw.

a) There are ——————————— ice cream cones.

b) There are ——————— tomatoes.

c) There are ——————— candies.

d) There are ——————— beans.

1 Write **E** for even numbers and **O** for odd numbers in the hula-hoops below.

Desenhorama

AFTER THIS UNIT I CAN

Ask and answer questions.

Recognize toys, games, and words related to amusement parks.

Use question words.

Recognize and write numbers from 20-59.

Understand the difference between even and odd numbers.

Understand the history of hula-hoops.

UNIT 3

THE FARM

It is my **first** time on a **farm**. It is very interesting!

Yes, it is! We **can** have fun with **horses**, **chickens**, and **pigs**.

Dylan, look! There is a horse!

I love **ducks** and **rabbits**!

Wow, it is a big one!

VOCABULARY

Can: podemos (poder).
Chicken(s): galinha(s).
Duck(s): pato(s).
Farm: fazenda.

First: primeira.
Horse(s): cavalo(s).
Pig(s): porco(s).
Rabbit(s): coelho(s).

1 Where are the kids?

a)  ☐ In a zoo.

b)  ☐ On a farm.

c)  ☐ In a park.

2 Complete the crossword with the name of the animals that live on the farm.

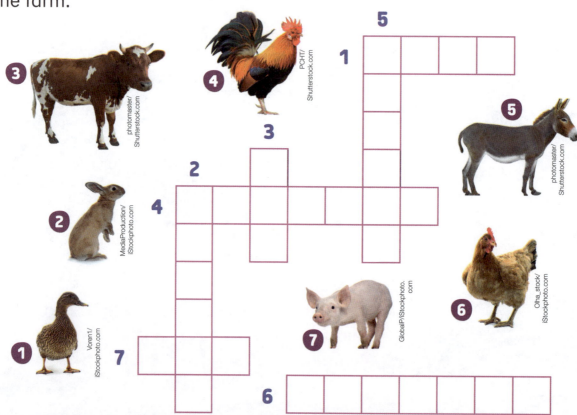

3 Unscramble the letters to find out the name of the animals.

a) HSEOR

_____

b) WCO

_____

c) CKDU

_____

d) EPSHE

_____

e) TBRBAI

_____

f) GIP

_____

g) NCEHKIC

_____

h) KNEOYD

_____

4 Who am I? Match and name the shadows appropriately.

Lexi Claus/Shutterstock

Affirmative sentences

Bob = He
Bob **likes** ducks.
He **likes** ducks.
Emma = She
Emma **likes** rabbits.
She **likes** rabbits.

I like ducks.   I like rabbits.

Vanessa Alexandre

LET'S PLAY

1 What is the appropriate form of the verb? Choose the best option and complete the sentences.

a) I _____ pigs.

☐ like
☐ likes

b) Dylan _____ sheep.

☐ like
☐ likes

c) I _____ horses.

☐ like
☐ likes

d) Bob _____ donkeys.

☐ like
☐ likes

GOOD DEED

Educating children about animal care

Make a drawing of a farm animal that you like.

LET'S HAVE FUN

1 Play of imitating the animals!

I went to visit a farm one day

I went to visit a farm one day,
I saw a cow **across the way**,
And what do you think I **heard** it say?
MOO, MOO, MOO! MOO, MOO, MOO!

I **went** to visit a farm one day,
I **saw** a sheep across the way,
And what do you think I heard it **say**?
BAA, BAA, BAA! BAA, BAA, BAA!

I went to visit a farm one day,
I saw a pig across the way,
And what do you **think** I heard it say?
OINK, OINK, OINK! OINK, OINK, OINK!

Traditional nursery rhyme.

VOCABULARY

Across the way: do outro lado.
Heard (to hear): ouvi (ouvir).
Saw (to see): vi (ver).
Say (to say): dizer.
Think (to think): acha (achar).
Went (to go): fui (ir).

Marcos de Mello

The horses are on the farms or little farms

Let's make a research about horses. Then write a sentence with what you found.

ENGLISH AROUND THE WORLD

The technology used in agriculture around the world

Where is the drone? Circle the appropriate picture.

1 Listen to Bob and Brad talking and circle all the animals mentioned.

2 What farm animal is their favorite? Listen to the kids and mark the answer as they speak. Then, stick the picture of the animal.

a) Natasha likes...

☐ rabbits. ☐ sheep.

b) Lisa likes...

☐ donkeys. ☐ ducks.

c) Brad likes...

☐ cows. ☐ horses.

d) Clair likes...

☐ rabbits. ☐ chickens.

LET'S HAVE FUN

1 Look at the pictures and mark 10 differences between them.

Lexi Claus/Shutterstock

AFTER THIS UNIT I CAN

Talk about animals.

Identify farm animals.

Understand how much care animals need every day.

Identify the importance of farm animals.

Understand the importance of using technology on farms.

UNIT 4

OUR WINTER VACATION

It's winter. Bob, Lisa, Stephany, and Brad are on vacation.

That's a **good idea**! Let's **sled**!

Let's go **play** in the **snow**!

The **winter** is very **cold**.

Let's **make** a **snowman**!

VOCABULARY

Cold: frio.

Good: boa.

Idea: ideia.

Make (to make): fazer.

Play (to play): brincar.

Sled (to sled): escorregar, deslizar de trenó.

Snow: neve.

Snowman: boneco de neve.

Winter: inverno.

Vanessa Alexandre

1 The kids are on vacation. Check the correct season and paste the stickers.

☐ Spring

☐ Winter

☐ Summer

☐ Autumn/Fall

2 What does Brad want to do?

☐ Go skiing.

☐ Do sledding.

3 What are the children wearing? Draw.

1 Look at the picture and read the text about the seasons.

Plan for your perfect adventure in any season

Winter (15°-42° F / -9°- 5° C): Temperatures drop, and the region becomes a winter wonderland glittering with radiant ice and snow. Too cold? Visit one of the many indoor attractions.

What to pack: beanies, a scarf, a warm coat, mittens, winter boots, travel mug.

Spring (35°-76° F / 1°-24° C): When spring has sprung, it's time to get outside and explore. Hit the trails, attend an outdoor concert or festival, or plan a picnic.

Niagara Falls, USA.

What to pack: sunglasses, hat, poncho, warm coat, hiking boots, picnic basket.

Summer (56°-81° F / 13°-27° C): Expect warm weather and plenty of sunshine. Cool off on the water, or visit a local ice cream shop for a hand-scooped cone.

What to pack: sunglasses, hat, poncho, water bottle, water shoes, sunblock.

Fall (35°-76° F / 1°-24° C): There is nothing about falling at the Falls. Think u-pick farms, a vibrantly colored landscape, and an unearthly share of spooky spectacles.

What to pack: hat, travel mug, light jacket, camera, hiking boots, binoculars.

Geneva Walker. *Niagara Falls - Travel Guide 2023-2024.* [S. l.: s. n.], [2023].

2 Which season do you prefer? Write.

_____

3 Which of these items do you need in the winter? Color.

Opposite adjectives

hot

cold

happy

sad

fast

slow

young

old

big

small

Get to know Niagara Falls and Skylon Tower in Canada

In what season doesn't the cable car operate at Skylon Tower?

___

ENGLISH AROUND THE WORLD

Winter Olympic Games

Check the words related to winter.

- [ ] Snow
- [ ] Hot
- [ ] Cold
- [ ] Summer
- [ ] Sun
- [ ] Falls

1 What do they like about winter? Listen and match.

a)

Dylan

b)

Natasha

c)

Bruce

d)

Clair

2 What about you? Draw what you like to do in winter.

GOOD DEED

Let's protect the animals during the winter

We must take care of our pets and street animals.

What do you need to do to protect the animals in winter? Write.

_____

I am a little snowman

I'm a **little snowman**,
short and fat.
Made from **little snowflakes**
that **fell** to the **ground**
Here's my **tummy**.
Here's my hat.
I'm all snow from head to **toe**!

I'm a little snowman,
short and fat.
Made from little snowflakes
that fell to the ground
Raisins for my eyes,
And a carrot nose,
I'm all snow from head to toe!

Traditional nursery rhyme.
Adapted.

Vanessa Alexandre

 VOCABULARY

Fell (to fall): caíram (cair).
Ground: chão.
Little: pequeno(s).
Raisin(s): uva(s)-passa(s).
Snowflake(s): floco(s) de neve.
Snowman: boneco de neve.
Toe: dedo do pé.
Tummy: barriga.

LET'S LISTEN

1 Listen and check the correct option. Then complete the sentences.

a) He is ______________.

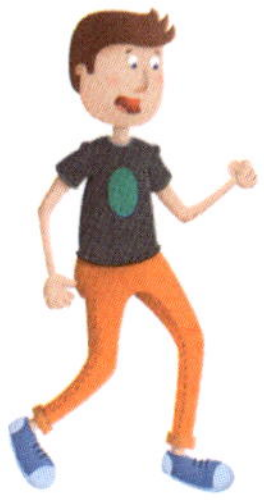
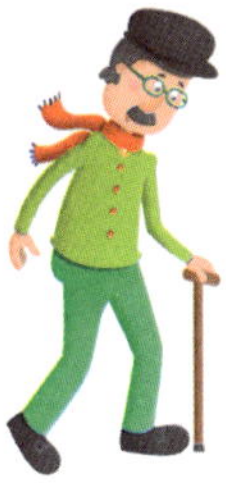

Carolina Sartório

- [ ] young
- [ ] old

b) Turtles are ______________.

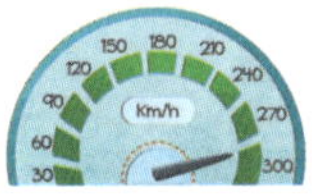

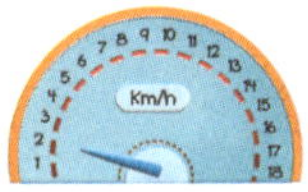

Carolina Sartório

- [ ] fast
- [ ] slow

c) It is a ______________ house.

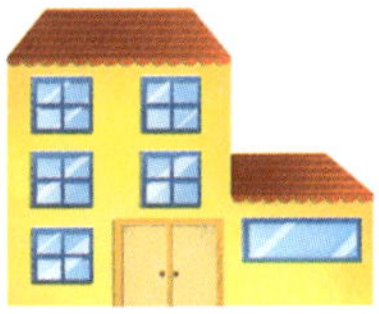
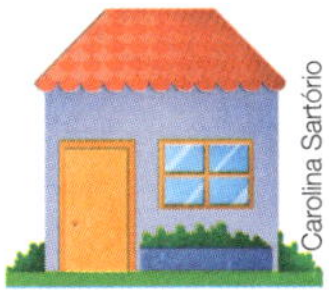

Carolina Sartório

- [ ] small
- [ ] big

d) Today is ______________.

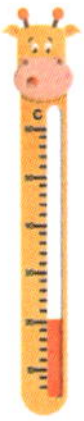
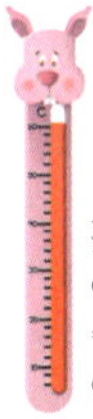

Carolina Sartório

- [ ] hot
- [ ] cold

e) I am ______________ today.

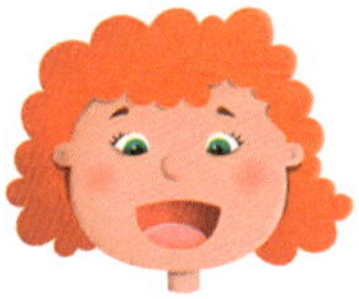
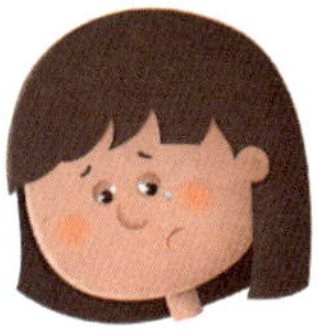

Carolina Sartório

- [ ] happy
- [ ] sad

1 Count and circle the kids playing in the snow, then check.

| ☐ Ten | ☐ Five | ☐ Four | ☐ Fourteen |

AFTER THIS UNIT I CAN

	😊	😐	☹
Ask people questions and reply to theirs.	◯	◯	◯
Identify the seasons of the year.	◯	◯	◯
Identify different types of winter vacation.	◯	◯	◯
Understand how to take care of animals in winter.	◯	◯	◯
Identify Winter Olympics sports.	◯	◯	◯

5 HEALTHY FOOD

My favorite fruits are **watermelon**, **strawberry**, and **orange**.

Yes, I like it. But I don't like **fried chicken**.

Do you like **roast** chicken for **lunch**?

What **healthy foods** do you like?

I **like fruits** and **fish**.

Remember that it is important to wash your hands before every **meal**.

I **love** fruit salad.

Hum! I like steak and **vegetables** for **dinner**.

Vanessa Alexandre

VOCABULARY

Chicken: frango.
Dinner: jantar.
Fish: peixe.
Food(s): alimento(s).
Fried: frito.
Fruit(s): fruta(s).

Healthy: saudáveis.
Like (to like): gosto (gostar).
Love (to love): amo (amar).
Lunch: almoço.
Meal: refeição.

Orange: laranja.
Roast: assado.
Strawberry: morango.
Vegetable(s): verdura(s) e legume(s).
Watermelon: melancia.

COMPREHENSION

1 What are Johnny's favorite fruits?

Vanessa Alexandre

_____
_____
_____

2 Which foods do they like? Match.

a) Johnny

b) Bill

Steak and vegetables

foodandstyle/iStockphoto.com

Fruits

Adcharin/iStockphoto.com

3 Which healthy foods do you like? Color and write their names.

graphixmania/Shutterstock.com

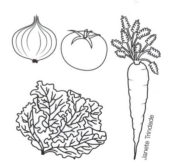

Janete Trindade

_____   _____

NikWB/Shutterstock.com

vectortatu/Shutterstock.com

_____   _____

1 Color each fruit according to the color indicated.

a) A yellow banana.

Ilustrações: Janete Trindade

b) A red apple.

c) A green pear.

d) An orange peach.

e) A yellow papaya.

f) A red strawberry.

2 Unscramble the letters and find out the names of some healthy foods.

a) AKBDE OTAPOT:

_____

b) ASTKE:

_____

c) SLADA:

_____

d) NAGOER UCEJI:

_____

e) GGES:

_____

f) IFSH:

_____

3 Match each fruit to its corresponding picture.

a) pineapple

Nguyen Dinh Minh Quan/iStockphoto.com

b) watermelon

Viktor Ahelev/iStockphoto.com

c) strawberry

Roman Samokhin/ iStockphoto.com

d) peach

anilakkus/iStockphoto.com

Access to healthy food is a child's right

Paste the stickers in the correct column.

Healthy Food	Non-Healthy Food

ABC GRAMMAR POINT

Modal verb – Would

Would is used to make polite questions or requests.

What would you like to order?

I would like some pasta, please.

I would like a sandwich, please.

Vanessa Alexandre

LET'S PLAY

1 Fill in the blanks with the modal verb **would**.

Waiter: What_____you like to order?

Brad: I_____like a lasagna and a pineapple juice, please.

Clair: I_____like a hamburger and french fries, please.

2 What would they like to order? Complete the requests.

a) I _____ like a lettuce, carrot, and tomato salad, please.

b) I _____ like a steak and some potatoes, please.

Apple tree

Apple tree
Swing with me
Underneath the apple tree,
We will swing,
We will sing,
Till the dinner **bell**.
To and fro we will go,
Flying to the sky,
Happily, **merrily**, up we **swing**,
With the birds we'll fly.

Nursery rhyme.

VOCABULARY

Bell: sino.
Flying (to fly): voando (voar).
Happily: alegremente.
Merrily: alegremente.

Swing (to swing): balançamos (balançar).
Till: até.
To and fro: para lá e para cá.
Underneath: embaixo.

Marcos de Mello

Typical foods

Look at the pictures. Name each country and its typical food.

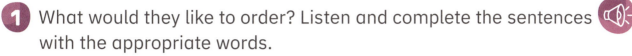

LET'S LISTEN

1 What would they like to order? Listen and complete the sentences   with the appropriate words.

a) Bill would like to order _____ and a baked potato.

JoeGough/iStockphoto.com

b) Lisa would like to order _____ and steak.

gbh007/iStockphoto.com

c) Stephany would like to order _____ , lettuce, and tomato.

kivoart/iStockphoto.com

d) Brad would like to order _____, salad, rice, and beans.

Hilario Junior/iStockphoto.com

DIGITAL PLAY

Let's buy healthy food!

Research and write the prices.

Shopping list

Fruits _____

Vegetables _____

Carrot _____

Lettuce _____

Tomato _____

Spinach _____

Onion _____

Garlic _____

Orange _____

Lemon _____

Grape _____

Pineapple _____

Avocado _____

Apple _____

Milk _____

Cheese _____

Bread _____

Natural fruit juice _____

Bean _____

Rice _____

Cereal _____

AFTER THIS UNIT I CAN

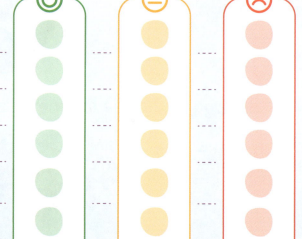

Ask people questions and reply to theirs.

Talk about healthy and unhealthy foods.

Identify different fruits, vegetables, and meat.

Identify colors.

Recognize the importance of healthy eating as a right.

Establish a commitment to healthy eating.

Use numbers in a real situation.

6 A VISIT TO STEPHANY'S HOUSE

Hi, **guys**! **Welcome** to my house!

It's my **home, sweet home**.

Good morning, Stephany!

And it's big, too!

It's a beautiful house, Stephany!

Vanessa Alexandre

📖 VOCABULARY

Guys: pessoal.
Home, sweet home: lar, doce lar.
Welcome: bem-vindos.

1 Where are the kids? Check.

  ☐ At Lisa's house.

  ☐ At Brad's house.

  ☐ At Stephany's house.

2 What time of day is it? Circle.

At night.　　　In the morning.　　　In the afternoon.

3 Trace the words.

Home
Sweet
Home

4 How is Stephany's house? Check.

- [ ] It's big.
- [ ] It's ugly.
- [ ] It's sweet.
- [ ] It's beautiful.
- [ ] It's small.
- [ ] It's boring.

5 How is your home? Draw it.

LET'S PLAY

1 What room is this? Look and choose a word from the box to name the room.

living room ✳ laundry ✳ bedroom
garage ✳ bathroom ✳ dining room
attic ✳ kitchen

a)

_____

b)

_____

c)

_____

d)

_____

e)

_____

f)

_____

g)

_____

h)

_____

2 Find ten house rooms in the wordsearch.

B	E	D	R	O	O	M	M	E	A	C	H	A	L	L
A	J	W	P	O	Y	U	Y	D	T	P	X	Y	U	I
S	S	G	A	R	A	G	E	N	T	J	M	E	J	V
E	T	D	K	Y	B	V	C	F	I	B	C	A	S	I
M	Q	N	C	I	I	K	I	T	C	H	E	N	A	N
E	A	F	P	A	J	L	P	G	*	U	P	A	O	G
N	H	K	K	B	A	T	H	R	O	O	M	H	D	*
T	X	P	V	P	G	F	K	D	L	V	P	G	G	R
A	R	D	I	N	I	N	G	*	R	O	O	M	X	O
F	E	*	T	F	K	L	V	A	J	L	P	G	Y	O
H	D	N	L	A	U	N	D	R	Y	*	R	O	O	M

bedroom
garage
kitchen
bathroom
dining room
laundry room
hall
living room
basement
attic

3 Write about your house or apartment using the words in the box.

big ✱ green ✱ brown ✱ old ✱ blue ✱ ugly

orange ✱ black ✱ small

purple ✱ pink ✱ yellow ✱ new ✱ red

beautiful ✱ white

My home is _____

_____

_____

_____

_____

_____

_____

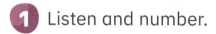
1 Listen and number.

☐ bedroom

☐ dining room

☐ bathroom

☐ basement

☐ kitchen

☐ attic

☐ hall

☐ laundry

☐ living room

☐ garage

E-waste pollution and the environment

Circle the e-waste.

laptop	television	bottle	earphones	pencil
cell phone	shoes	food	clothes	battery

Let's recycle!

Gather cans, bottles, paper, books, and plastic. These materials can be recycled. Reuse stuff. Let's save the planet!

Paste the stickers in the correct trash bin.

E-WASTE   PLASTIC   METAL   GLASS   PAPER   ORGANIC

When Goldilocks went to the house of the bears

When **Goldilocks went** to the house of the **bears**,
Oh, what did her two eyes **see**?
A **bowl** that was **huge**,
A bowl that was **small**,
A bowl that was **tiny** and that was **all**,
She counted them: one, two, three.
When Goldilocks went to the house of the bears,
Oh, what did her two eyes see?
A **chair** that was huge,
A chair that was small,
A chair that was tiny and that was all,

VOCABULARY

All: tudo.
Bear(s): urso(s).
Bed: cama.
Bowl: tigela.
Chair: cadeira.
Counted (to count): contou (contar).
Goldilocks: Cachinhos Dourados.

Growled (to growl): rosnaram (rosnar).
Huge: enorme.
See (to see): viram (ver).
Small: pequeno(a).
Tiny: minúsculo(a).
Went (to go): foi (ir).

She **counted** them: one, two, three.
When Goldilocks went to the house of the bears,
Oh, what did her two eyes see?
A **bed** that was huge,
A bed that was small,
A bed that was tiny and that was all,
She counted them: one, two, three.
When Goldilocks ran from the house of the bears,
Oh, what did her two eyes see?

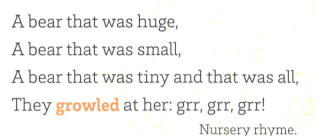

A bear that was huge,
A bear that was small,
A bear that was tiny and that was all,
They **growled** at her: grr, grr, grr!

Nursery rhyme.

Marcos de Mello

E-waste management: We must protect our home!

On October 14, International E-Waste Day highlights the urgent importance of recycling electronic devices amidst the escalating global problem of electronic waste, commonly known as e-waste.

Do you recycle electronics at home? Mark.

☐ Yes.

☐ No.

1 Listen and answer the questions.

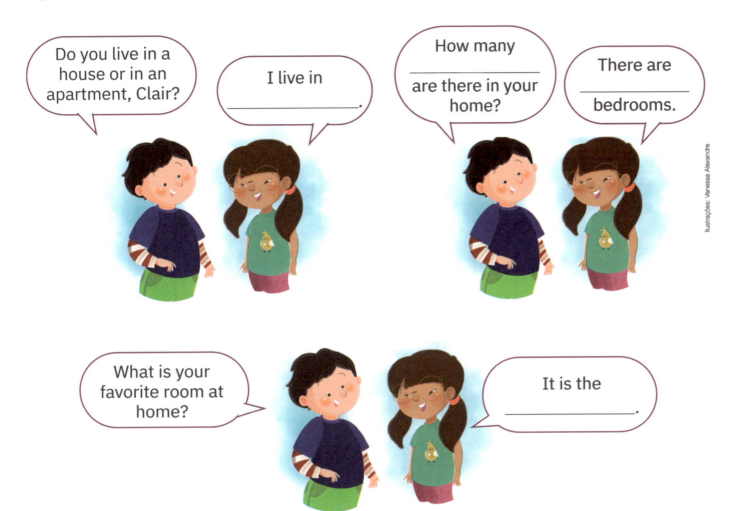

Do you live in a house or in an apartment, Clair?

I live in _____.

How many _____ are there in your home?

There are _____ bedrooms.

What is your favorite room at home?

It is the _____.

Ilustrações: Vanessa Alexandre

2 Complete the sentences and practice the dialogue with a classmate.

Student A: Do you live in a house or in an apartment?

Student B: I live in _____. What about you?

Student A: I live in _____.

Student A: How many _____ are there in your home?

Student B: There are _____ .

Student A: What is your favorite room at home?

Student B: It is _____.

1 Help the girl get to her bedroom.

Reinaldo Rosa

AFTER THIS UNIT I CAN

Recognize adjectives.

Identify the periods of the day: morning, afternoon, and night.

Identify the rooms of the house.

Recognize the importance of recycling.

Talk about electronic waste.

Hello, class! Let's **learn** about the human **body**! Look at this picture. This is a human body. These are the **head**, the **hair**, the **eyes**, the **ears**, the **nose**, the **mouth**, the **shoulders**, the **arms**, the **hands**, the **belly**, the **legs**, and the **feet**.

Vanessa Alexandre

VOCABULARY

Arm(s): braço(s).
Belly: barriga.
Body: corpo.
Ear(s): orelha(s).
Eye(s): olho(s).

Feet: pés.
Hair: cabelo.
Hand(s): mão(s).
Head: cabeça.
Learn (to learn): aprender.

Leg(s): perna(s).
Mouth: boca.
Nose: nariz.
Shoulder(s): ombro(s).

1 Where are the students? What is the theme of the class?

☐ In a classroom. / Human body.

☐ In a cafeteria. / Healthy food.

2 Look at the picture and name the parts of the body.

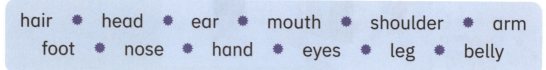

hair ✳ head ✳ ear ✳ mouth ✳ shoulder ✳ arm
foot ✳ nose ✳ hand ✳ eyes ✳ leg ✳ belly

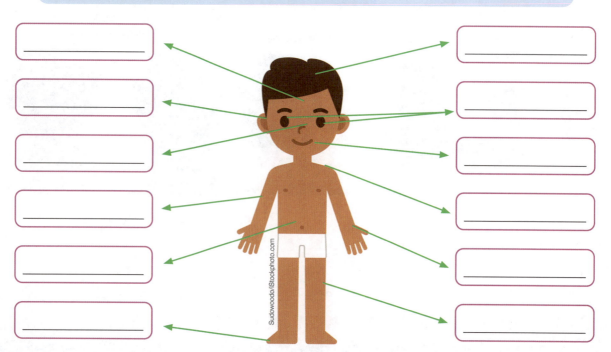

1 Observe the pictures. Read and say the names of the body parts.

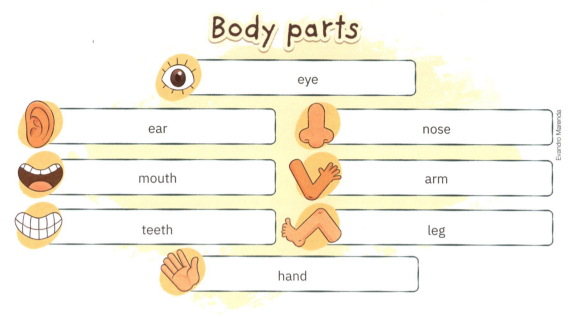

Body parts

eye

ear

nose

mouth

arm

teeth

leg

hand

Evandro Marenda

2 Write a sentence with one of the body parts above.

_____

3 Check the photos that represent good body care.

evgenyatamanenko/iStockphoto.com

m-gucci/iStockphoto.com

FG Trade/iStockphoto.com

Yana Tatevosian/iStockphoto.com

4 Find ten human body parts in the wordsearch.

shoulder	✳	foot	✳	hand	✳	belly	✳	nose
ear	✳	mouth	✳	arm	✳	head	✳	eye

E	S	D	N	O	S	E	K	L	Q	W	E	T	R	R
A	Y	B	F	G	H	Y	G	H	B	E	L	L	Y	T
R	L	F	J	M	Z	E	M	G	H	C	S	E	C	H
L	S	E	D	O	G	F	E	Z	N	B	X	A	C	J
A	Q	T	D	U	X	H	A	N	D	Y	T	R	A	K
W	F	A	Q	T	T	A	A	Z	S	J	I	O	R	C
A	N	D	L	H	R	T	P	S	X	K	H	A	M	B
Y	B	F	G	H	F	O	O	T	E	K	E	Y	F	V
K	E	H	B	I	L	W	E	N	X	H	A	A	P	M
S	H	O	U	L	D	E	R	O	E	R	D	G	X	P

5 Complete the words with the missing letters.

a) HE _____ D

b) S _____ OUL _____ ER

c) F _____ OT

d) _____ OUTH

e) E _____ R

f) _____ YE

g) B _____ LL _____

h) A _____ M

i) N _____ S _____

j) H _____ I _____

k) H _____ N _____

LET'S LISTEN

1 Listen, repeat, and number the body parts.

Carolina Sartório

Hand washing song

Wash hands well each day,
To **keep** germs **away**.
Scrub with soap and water,
And **be on your way**.
Wash hands well each day,
To keep germs away.
Scrub with soap and water,
And be on your way.

Nursery rhyme.

Marcos de Mello

VOCABULARY

Away: longe.

Be on your way (to be on your way): siga seu caminho (seguir seu caminho).

Keep (to keep): manter.

Scrub (to scrub): esfregue (esfregar).

Wash (to wash): lave (lavar).

Ways to say thank you in English

✏️ Write your favorite form to say thank you.

_____

_____

_____

▶️ **DIGITAL PLAY**

Discover the Powerhouse Museum in Australia

Mark the senses that an art immersion can explore in the body.

- ☐ sight
- ☐ hearing
- ☐ hunger
- ☐ taste

- ☐ smell
- ☐ pain
- ☐ touch

LET'S LISTEN

1 Listen to Clair. Circle the body part she hurt.

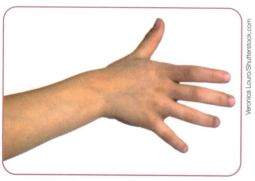

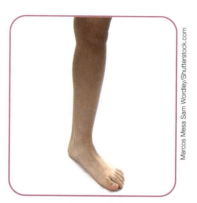

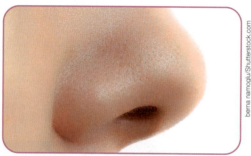

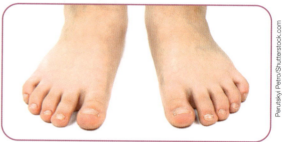

2 Listen to Clair again. Make an **X** in the place where she hurt herself.

   ☐ In the classroom.

   ☐ On a soccer game.

   ☐ At the museum.

Taking care of our body

It's very important to take care of our body. Have a healthy diet and practice sports.

How do you take good care of your body? Make a drawing to illustrate a very good habit for your health.

fizkes/iStockphoto.com

LET'S PLAY

1 Create a comic strip and paste the stickers.

2 Find 5 differences in the picture.

Ksenya Savva/Shutterstock.com

3 Complete the crossword.

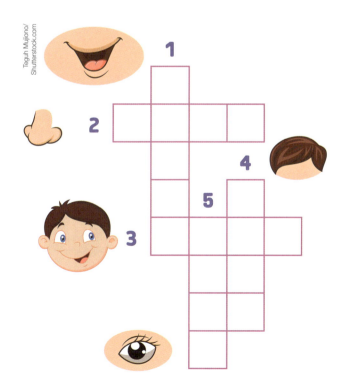

Teguh Mujiono/
Shutterstock.com

1

2

4

5

3

4 Match the senses to the body parts.

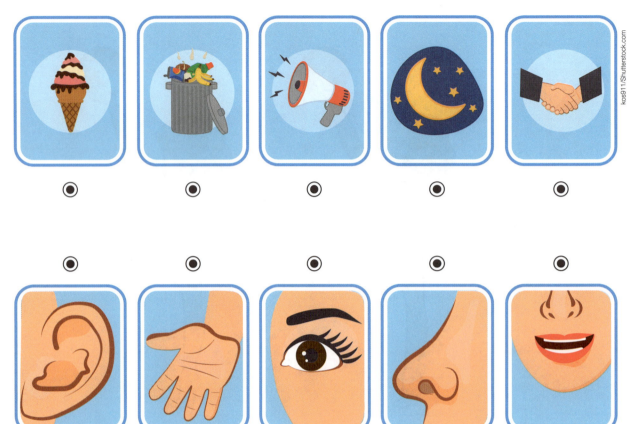

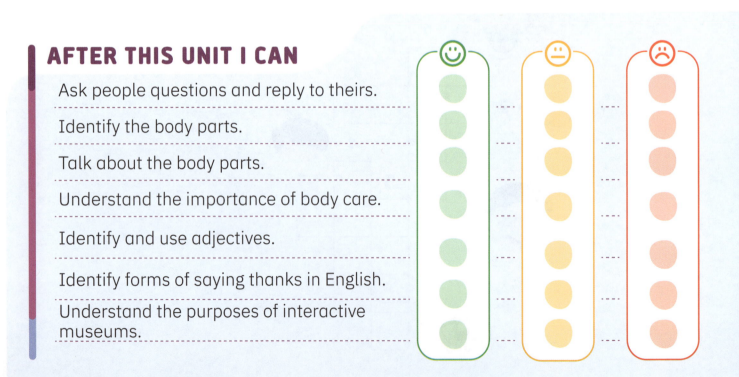

AFTER THIS UNIT I CAN

Ask people questions and reply to theirs.

Identify the body parts.

Talk about the body parts.

Understand the importance of body care.

Identify and use adjectives.

Identify forms of saying thanks in English.

Understand the purposes of interactive museums.

8 THE MASQUERADE

> Hello, class! This **week** we are **preparing** a **masquerade**! We **need** to **make some masks** and **choose** the **costumes**.

> Teacher, this is cool!

> I **love** costumes! Princess, ladybug, angel, and butterfly are my favorite costumes.

> The masquerade will be amazing!

> And I **like** the pirate, policeman, cowboy, and clown costumes.

Vanessa Alexandre

 VOCABULARY

Choose (to choose): escolher.

Costume(s): fantasia(s).

Like (to like): gosto (gostar).

Love (to love): amo (amar).

Make (to make): fazer.

Mask(s): máscara(s).

Masquerade: baile de máscaras.

Need (to need): precisamos (precisar).

Preparing (to prepare): preparando (preparar).

Some: alguns/algumas.

Week: semana.

1 Check the picture according to the audio. What are the kids and the teacher preparing?

☐ A masquerade.   ☐ A birthday party.

2 What do the kids need to wear to the masquerade? Circle.

A mask

A T-shirt

A cap

A costume

1 What costume is this? Match to the corresponding image.

a) butterfly

b) princess

c) pirate

d) policeman

e) cowboy

f) clown

g) angel

h) ladybug

2 Complete the crossword puzzle with the costumes below.

1

Michelle D. Milliman/
Shutterstock.com

2

Alena Kazlouskaya/Shutterstock.com

3

KellyBoreson/Shutterstock.com

4

Veronica Louro/Shutterstock.com

5

Oksana Kuzmina/Shutterstock.com

6

MG Best For You/Shutterstock.com

7

aldegonde/Shutterstock.com

Question words

What – O quê ✷ **When** – Quando ✷ **Where** – Onde

Observe:

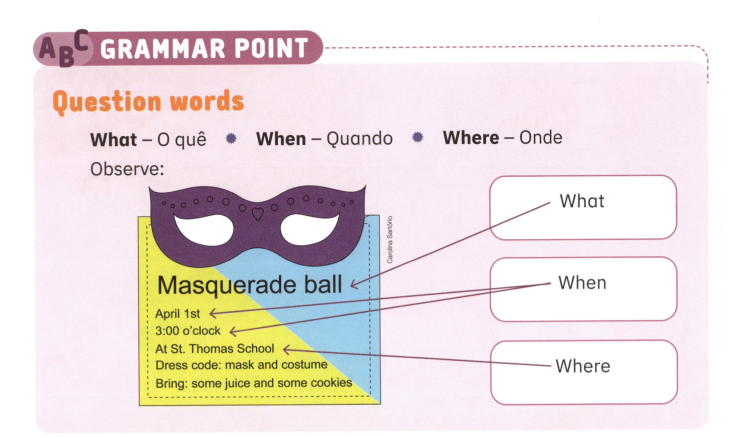

Masquerade ball

April 1st
3:00 o'clock
At St. Thomas School
Dress code: mask and costume
Bring: some juice and some cookies

What

When

Where

Carolina Sartório

LET'S LISTEN

1 Listen and complete with the information about the masquerade.

Vectors Bang/
Shutterstock.com

Masquerade

When?

_____

Where?

_____

What time?

_____

Dress code:

_____

What to bring:

_____

Hey, diddle diddle

Hey, diddle diddle,
The cat and the **fiddle**,
The cow **jumped over** the **moon**,
The little dog **laughed** to see such sport,
And the **dish ran away** with the **spoon**.

Traditional nursery rhyme.

VOCABULARY

Dish: prato.
Fiddle: violino.
Jumped (to jump): pulou (pular).
Laughed (to laugh): riu (rir).
Moon: lua.
Over: por cima.
Ran away (to run away): fugiu (fugir).
Spoon: colher.

LET'S LISTEN

1 What costume do they want to wear? Listen and circle their choices.

Desenhorama

Natasha and Brad are buying costumes for the masquerade.

Look! There _____ butterfly, _____ , ladybug, and Little Red Riding Hood _____ . I choose the butterfly _____ for the _____ . What about you?

There are _____ , cowboy, clown, and _____ costumes. I want to wear the _____ costume.

Ilustrações: Vanessa Alexandre

3 What costume would you like to wear at the masquerade? Draw it.

Masquerades and costume parties!

Look at the pictures and answer the questions.

 a)

What party is this? _____

Where is it? _____

When does this party happen? _____

 b)

What is this? _____

Where is it? _____

When does this happen? _____

c)

What is this? _____

Where is this? _____

When does this happen? _____

d)

What is this? _____

Where is this? _____

When does this happen? _____

1 Look at the image and count the masks.

2 Find the 7 differences at the masquerade.

Ilustrações: Vanessa Alexandre

Let's have our masquerade and costume party!

AFTER THIS UNIT I CAN

Write an invitation.

Identify the elements of a masquerade.

Recognize different costumes.

Use question words.

Find out about celebrations and costume parties from around the world (Italy, the United States, Mexico, and Brazil).

Understand that costume parties are cultural manifestations of the countries.

REVIEW

Unit 1

1 Count the musical instruments and write the number.

a) Guitar

RapidEye/iStockphoto.com

b) Violin

tarasov_vl/iStockphoto.com

c) Drums

YinYang/iStockphoto.com

d) Flute

EdnaM/iStockphoto.com

2 Write the name of your favorite musical instrument.

Unit 2

1 Circle the numbers from 20 to 59.

BINGO (blue)

17	20	38	32	16
48	1	24	59	39
42	35	⭐	33	14
37	4	3	20	54
32	55	45	11	45

BINGO (yellow)

48	32	38	24	56
58	20	13	15	54
58	55	⭐	50	33
5	35	47	55	56
52	34	48	36	57

BINGO (green)

13	11	14	30	12
36	42	16	24	1
13	42	⭐	33	35
27	23	34	23	13
28	9	41	48	38

BINGO (orange)

6	52	23	35	14
55	46	18	48	31
29	26	⭐	31	30
52	50	44	26	51
45	26	3	32	59

Unit 3

1 Circle and color only the farm animals.

2 Unscramble the letters and find farm animals.

a) IEHNKCC

_____

b) EEPSH

_____

c) OEHRS

_____

d) KYENDO

_____

e) KDCU

_____

Unit 4

1 Color only the winter items.

Artika95/Shutterstock.com

Unit 5

1 Write the name of four different fruits in the fruit basket.

Thomas Klee/Shutterstock.com

_____

2 Color your favorite fruit.

Des Mah/Shutterstock.com

   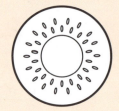

Unit 6

1 Name the parts of the house.

2 In what part of the house do you spend more time with your family?

_____

3 Match the different kinds of trash to the correct trash can.

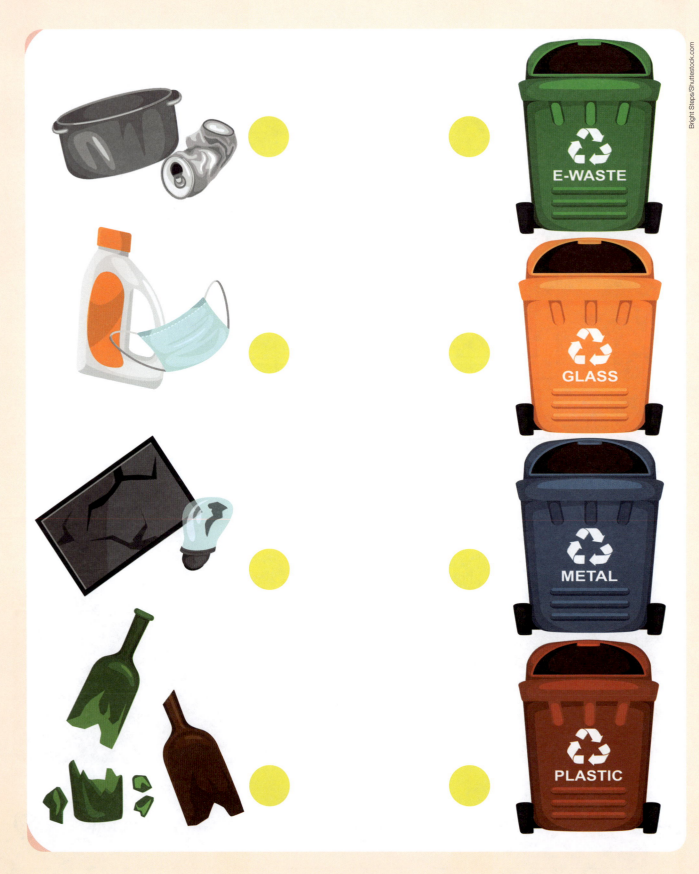

Unit 7

1 Complete the picture and write the names of the body parts.

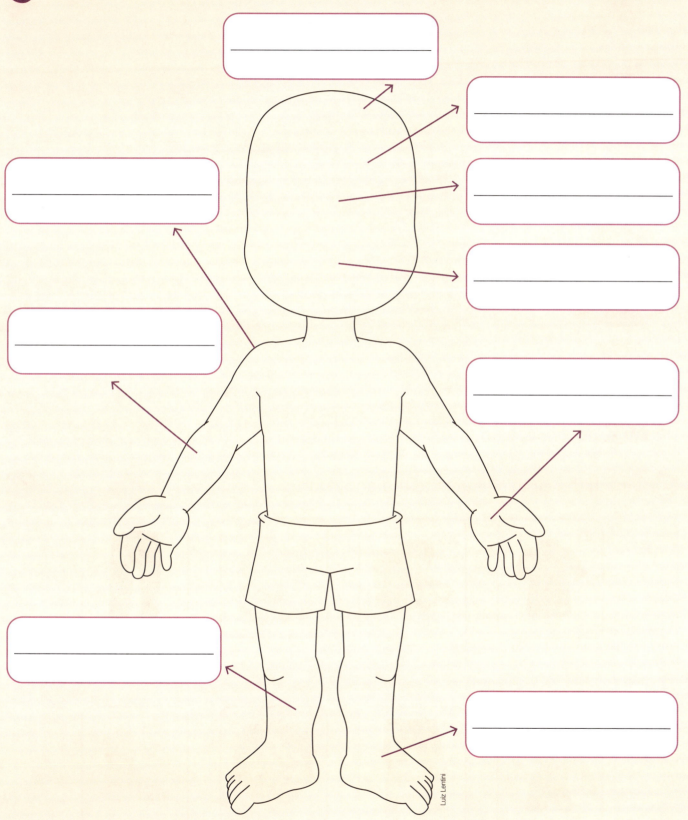

Match the picture to the corresponding body part. Then, trace the words.

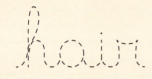

hair

mouth

nose

hand

3 Match the clothing items to the body parts.

   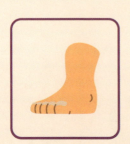

Unit 8

1 Join the dots and color.

2 Help the friends find each other in the masquerade.

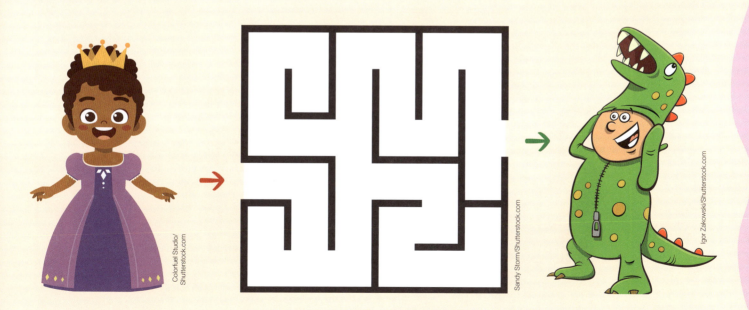

3 Circle the correct shadow. Then write the name of the costume.

arsansp/Shutterstock.com

a

arsansp/Shutterstock.com

b

idcreative.ddid/Shutterstock.com

c

idcreative.ddid/Shutterstock.com

d

idcreative.ddid/Shutterstock.com

Afternoon

Attic

Bathroom

Angel

Autumn

Bear

B

Apple

Banana

Bed

Arm

Basement

Bedroom

Big

Bird

Board

Bookshelf

Cap

Cat

Chair

Chicken

Classroom

Clown

Cold

Costume

Cow

Cowboy

Desk

Dining room

Dog

Donkey

Duck

E

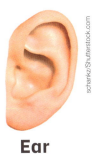

Ear

Elephant

Eraser

Eye

F

Fan

Farm

Fast

Fish

Foot

French fries

G

Garage

Giraffe

H

Hair

Hall

Hamster

Hand

Happy

Head

Horse

Hot

K

Kitchen

L

Lamp

Laundry

Leg

Library

Lion

Living room

M

Mask

Monkey

Morning

Mouth

N

Night

Nose

Notebook

O

Old

Orange

P

Papaya

Park

Pasta

Peach

Pear

Pen

Pencil

Pig

Pineapple

Pirate

Policeman

Princess

R

Rabbit

Ruler

S

Sad

Salad

Sandwich

Sharpener

Sheep

Shelf

Shoulder

Sink

Slow

Steak

T-shirt

Small

Strawberry

Turtle

W

Soda

Summer

Waiter

Sofa

T

Spring

Top

Wastebasket

Watermelon

Window

Winter

Young

Zoo

INDEX

SONGS

Lorelyn Medina/Shutterstock.com

LISTENINGS

Valentine's Day

From: _____

To: _____

Dobra

Easter

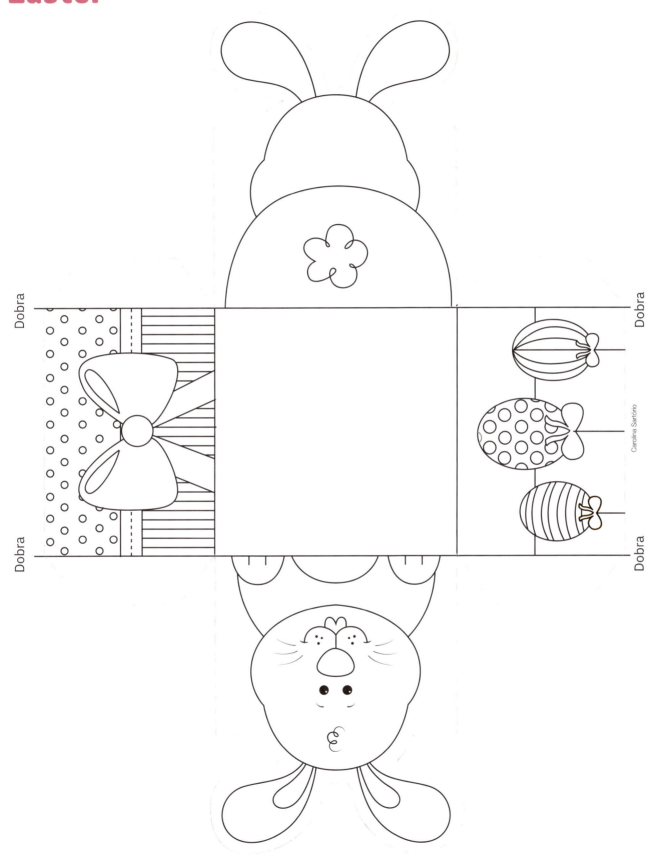

Carolina Sartório

Teacher's Day

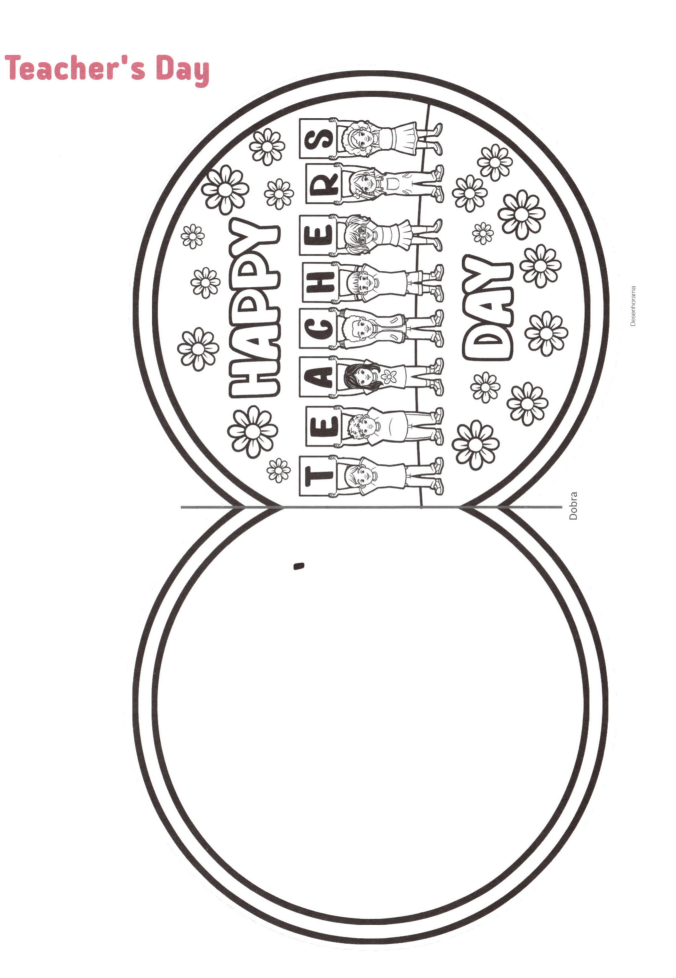

Desenhorama

Dobra

International Family's Day

Memorial Day

MEMORIAL DAY

—— REMEMBER AND HONOR ——

Dobra

Children's Day

Bruna Itsihara

Thanksgiving

Christmas

Carolina Sartório

Let's start!

Page 9

 Desenhorama

Unit 1

Page 25

CREATIVE **FRUSTRATED** **BORED** **THANKFUL**

Unit 2

Page 30

37 **52** **34** **59** **28** **40** **22** **31**

Unit 3

Page 49

 PeopleImages/iStockphoto.com

 Clara Bastian/iStockphoto.com

 vvvita/iStockphoto.com

 sergio_kumer/iStockphoto.com

Unit 4

Page 52

 mornay/iStockphoto.com

 AnaBGD/iStockphoto.com

 hobo_018/iStockphoto.com

 DaniloAndjus/iStockphoto.com

Unit 5

Page 65

vegetables

french fries

rice and beans

snacks

milk

stuffed cookie

fruit juice

soft drink

cheese

popcorn

fast food

fruits

Unit 6

Page 77

Unit 7

Page 92

Ilustrações: André Aguiar

Unit 8

Page 105